LIVING WITH MUM, LIVING WITH DAD

DAD

MUM

By Holly Duhig

BookLife
PUBLISHING

©2018
BookLife Publishing
King's Lynn
Norfolk PE30 4LS

A catalogue record for this
book is available from the
British Library.

ISBN: 978-1-78637-288-8

Written by:
Holly Duhig

Edited by:
Kirsty Holmes

Designed by:
Danielle Rippengill

All facts, statistics, web addresses and URLs in this book were verified as valid and accurate at time of writing.
No responsibility for any changes to external websites or references can be accepted by either the author or publisher.

Image Credits

All images are courtesy of Shutterstock.com, unless otherwise specified. With thanks to Getty Images, Thinkstock Photo and iStockphoto. Front Cover – wavebreakmedia, prapann, Alexander Lysenko, Mc Satori, Ian 2010, xpixel, Max Lashcheuski, pingebat, . Images used on every spread – Red_Spruce, MG Drachal, Alexander Lysenko, Kues, Flas100, Kanate, Nikolaeva. 1 – wavebreakmedia, prapann. 2 & 4 – wavebreakmedia. 5 – Ewelina Wachala, 1000 Words. 6 – Malykalexa. 7–11 – wavebreakmedia. 12 – kurhan. 13 – wavebreakmedia. 14 & 15 – Africa Studio. 16 – iordani. 16 & 17 – Photographee.eu. 18– 20 – wavebreakmedia. 21 – Cineberg. 22 & 23 – wavebreakmedia.

CONTENTS

WORDS THAT LOOK LIKE **THIS** CAN BE FOUND IN THE GLOSSARY ON PAGE 24.

My Family

My name is Anna, and this is my family. Here I am with my little brother, Luca, and our parents, Gael and Julia.

Although we are a family, we don't live all together anymore. A while ago, Mum and Dad decided to divorce, so now they live in different houses.

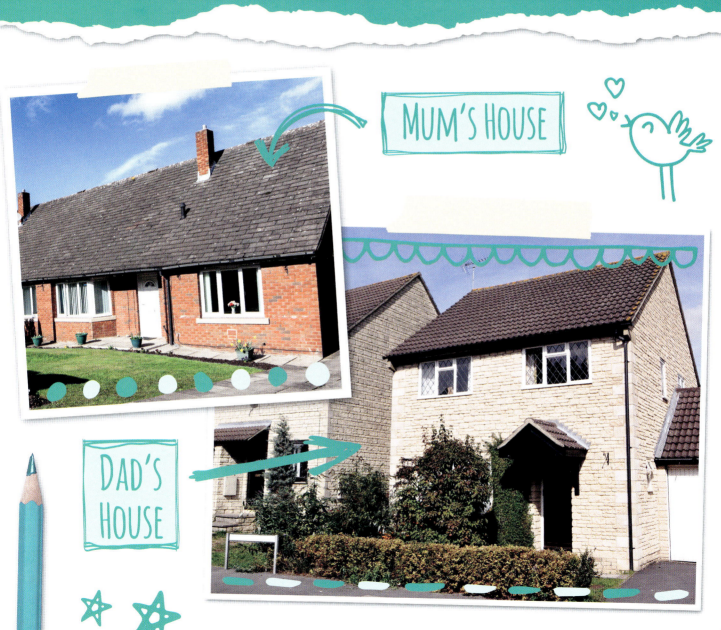

MUM'S HOUSE

DAD'S HOUSE

Living Apart

Divorce is when two people who were married decide they don't want to be married anymore.

You have to ask a **COURT** if you want to get divorced.

Divorce can be sad at first, but it is sometimes for the best.
Mum and Dad used to argue a lot. After a while, they realised
they would be happier if they lived apart.

My parents said they were **separating** because they were not in love with each other anymore. They both still love me and Luca very much though.

I didn't want Mum and Dad to divorce at first. I asked if they would ever get re-married again. Mum said they wouldn't, and that separating was for the best.

Feeling Sad 🙁

When Mum first told me and Luca that Dad was going to move out, I felt really sad and cried a lot. I was worried that Dad wanted to move out because of something I had done.

DIVORCE IS NEVER ANYONE'S FAULT.

I asked Dad if I wasn't being well-behaved enough. Dad told me that moving out was his decision and it would never be my fault, no matter how I behaved.

My Homes

WE ALL HELPED DAD MOVE IN.

Luca and I have two homes now. This is because Mum lives in our old house and Dad moved to a new house. Both of our homes are **unique**.

While Dad moved into his house, Luca and I lived with Mum. Now we live at Mum's one week and at Dad's the week after.

MUM AND DAD HAVE JOINT CUSTODY OF ME AND LUCA.

My best friend Callum goes to my **gymnastics** class. His parents are divorced too. He used to live with his mum but now he only lives with his dad.

CALLUM'S PARENTS HAVE BEEN DIVORCED FOR A WHILE.

CALLUM AND HIS DAD

Callum told me that moving house feels like moving into a new class with a new teacher. You might feel worried at first, but it soon feels normal.

My Bedrooms

My bedroom at Dad's house is very pretty. I try to keep it tidy.

It gets a bit messy when Luca and I play in it, though!

My bedroom at my Mum's house is pink too, and has a desk.
This is where I do my homework.

MISSING MUM AND MISSING DAD

AT LEAST I ALWAYS HAVE LUCA WITH ME!

Sometimes I miss Mum when I'm staying at Dad's house, and I miss Dad when I'm staying at Mum's house.

I used to worry that my parents would be upset if I told them I missed my other house, but they both understood.

DAD HELPS ME TALK TO MUM WHEN I'M AT HIS.

NEW BEGINNINGS

During the school holidays, Dad **introduced** me to his new girlfriend, Sarah. I felt really shy at first and I didn't want to speak to Sarah. I wanted to keep my dad all to myself.

After a while, though, I started speaking to Sarah more and more. She is a police officer so she has lots of cool stories.

I WANT TO BE A POLICE OFFICER ONE DAY TOO!

As time goes by, families grow and change. This can be a good thing. Mum and Dad are happier now than ever before.

AND AS FOR ME AND LUCA, WE EACH HAVE TWO BEDROOMS WITH TWO SETS OF TOYS AND GAMES!

Some families live together and some don't. But one thing's for sure – all families love each other very much.

Glossary and Index

Glossary

court	a place where legal decisions can be made
gymnastics	a type of exercise that improves strength and balance
introduced	to make someone known to another person
joint custody	an arrangement where parents who are divorced both look after a child and both give the child a home for some of the time
separating	to decide to live apart from a partner
unique	being the only one of its kind

Index